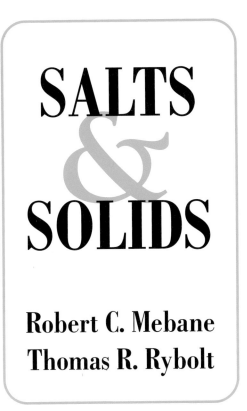

SALTS & SOLIDS

Robert C. Mebane

Thomas R. Rybolt

Illustrations by Anni Matsick

TWENTY-FIRST CENTURY BOOKS

A Division of Henry Holt and Company
New York

Twenty-First Century Books
A Division of Henry Holt and Company, Inc.
115 West 18th Street
New York, NY 10011

Henry Holt® and colophon are trademarks of
Henry Holt and Company, Inc.
Publishers since 1866

Library of Congress Cataloging-in-Publication Data

Mebane, Robert C.
Salts and solids / Robert C. Mebane and Thomas R. Rybolt;
illustrations by Anni Matsick.—1st ed.
p.   cm. — (Everyday material science experiments)
Includes bibliographical references and index.
1. Matter—Properties—Juvenile literature. 2. Matter—Experiments—
Juvenile literature. 3. Salts—Experiments—Juvenile literature.
4. Solids—Experiments—Juvenile literature. [1. Matter—Experiments.
2. Salts—Experiments. 3. Solids—Experiments. 4. Experiments.]
I. Rybolt, Thomas R. II. Matsick, Anni, ill., III. Title. IV. Series: Mebane,
Robert C. Everyday material science experiments.
QC173.16.M43   1995
530'.078—dc20   94–25201
                                                              CIP
                                                              AC

ISBN 0–8050–2841–2
First Edition 1995

Designed by Kelly Soong

Printed in Mexico
All first editions are printed on acid-free paper ∞.
10 9 8 7 6 5 4 3 2 1

For William, Katherine, Gunter, Peter, and Sadie

　　　　　　　　　　　　　　　　　　　　　—R.M.

*For my nephew, Will Garvin, and my nieces, Courtney Garvin
and Erin Garvin*

　　　　　　　　　　　　　　　　　　　　　—T.R.

ACKNOWLEDGMENT

We wish to thank Professor Mickey Sarquis of Miami University, Middletown, Ohio, for reading and making helpful comments on the manuscript.

CONTENTS

INTRODUCTION

The world around you is filled with *Air and Other Gases*, *Water and Other Liquids*, *Salts and Solids*, *Metals*, and *Plastics and Polymers*. Some of these materials are part of our natural environment; and some are part of our created, industrial environment. The materials that we depend on for life and the materials that are part of our daily living all have distinct properties. These properties can be best understood through careful examination and experimentation.

Have you ever wondered why plaster is hard, how an instant hot pack works, how a room can be soundproofed, or how carbon fibers can be made and used to make airplanes and rockets? In this book you will discover the answers to these and many other fascinating questions about *Salts and Solids*. In the process you will learn about salts and solids as materials—what they are made of, how they behave, and why they are important.

Each experiment is designed to stand alone. That is, it's not necessary to start with the first experiment and proceed to the second, then the third, and so on. Feel free to skip around—that's part of the fun of discovery. As you do the experiments, think about the results and what they mean to you. Also, think about how the results apply to the world around you.

At the beginning of each experiment, you will find one or more icons identifying the important physical science concepts dealt with in the experiment. For example, if the icon ❖ appears at the top of the page, it means that matter, one of the basic concepts of science, will be explored. On page 61 you will find a listing of all the icons—matter, energy, light, heat, sound, and electricity—and the experiments to which they relate.

As you carry out the experiments in this book, be sure to follow carefully any special safety instructions that are given. **For some experiments, a ❶ means that you should have an adult work with you.** For all your experiments, you need to make sure that an adult knows what you are doing. Remember to clean up after your experiment is completed.

DISAPPEARING SOLID

MATTER

MATERIALS NEEDED

Refrigerator freezer, frost-free

Paper towel

Water

Scissors

A liquid changes into a gas when the liquid evaporates. Normally we think of a solid first changing into a liquid and then the liquid changing into a gas. Do you think a solid could change directly into a gas without first changing into a liquid? In this experiment you will explore this possibility.

For this experiment you will need a frost-free refrigerator freezer. Nearly all modern refrigerator freezers are frost-free. A frost-free freezer is one that does not allow ice to build up on the inside of the compartment. The way a frost-free freezer works will be discussed later in the experiment.

Completely wet a sheet of paper towel with water. As shown in Figure A, squeeze the paper towel thoroughly to remove excess water. Unfold the towel, place it in the freezer, and leave it there overnight. You should find that the paper towel becomes completely frozen overnight. Leave the towel there for a week, continuing to check it each day. What happens to the frozen paper towel?

You should notice that after a day in the freezer, the paper towel starts to dry out. You may find that the paper towel becomes completely dry after just a few days in the freezer.

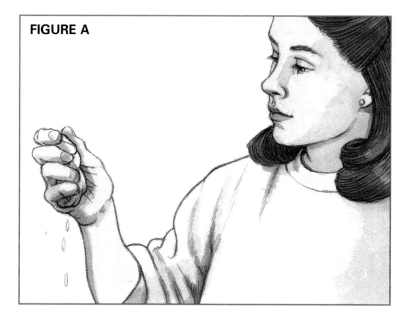

When you place the damp paper towel in the freezer, the water in the towel changes into ice. Ice is a solid consisting of frozen water molecules.

Water molecules in ice pack tightly together and are not free to move around because there is a strong attraction between the water molecules that are next to each other. Instead of moving around, water molecules in ice wiggle, or vibrate, in one spot. This is why ice is hard.

By absorbing energy from around them, water molecules on the surface of ice can vibrate quickly enough to break away from the strong attraction of their neighbors. When water molecules break away from the ice, they become a gas, or vapor. The process of a solid changing into a gas without first changing into a liquid is called *sublimation*.

The water molecules on the surface of the ice that escape as a gas become a part of the air in the freezer compartment. In frost-free freezers, a fan switches on periodically to pull the air out of the freezer compartment. This keeps the water vapor in the air of the freezer from changing back into frost on the cold surfaces inside the freezer. In an old freezer that is not frost-free, the water vapor inside the freezer condenses, or changes back into a solid, and can form thick layers of ice on the inside surfaces of the freezer.

In this experiment all the water that freezes in the paper towel *sublimes,* or changes into a vapor. This is why the paper towel becomes completely dry after a few days in the freezer.

Ice cubes that are old and have been in a frost-free freezer for a long period of time appear much smaller than newly formed ice cubes. The old ice cubes become smaller because frozen water molecules on the surface of the cubes sublime. Another common solid that undergoes sublimation is a mothball.

Freeze-drying is an important food preservation technique based on the sublimation of ice. Before the freeze-drying process begins, the food to be preserved is frozen solid. Next, the frozen food is placed in a vacuum, which speeds up the sublimation process. More than 90 percent of the water originally in the food is removed during the freeze-drying process. With the addition of water, freeze-dried foods regain much of their original shape, texture, and taste.

Astronauts and backpackers have been using freeze-dried foods for years. Once rather costly, freeze-dried foods can now be found in most grocery stores. Commonly found in grocery stores are freeze-dried coffee, soup mixes, and noodle mixes. Can you find other examples of freeze-dried food in a grocery store?

CHANGING A SOLID TO A LIQUID

MATERIALS NEEDED

Oven

Measuring spoons

Table sugar

Two aluminum pie pans

Table salt

Oven mitt

Hot pads

---

❶ **Alert! Adult supervision is needed.**

Which solid do you think is easier to change into a liquid, table salt or sugar? In this experiment you will find out.

Turn on the oven and set its temperature to 450°F (232°C). While the oven is heating, add 1 tablespoon of table sugar to an aluminum pie pan. Gently shake the pie pan sideways to cover the bottom of the pan evenly with sugar. Take the second pie pan, and bend a portion of its edge upward so that you will be able to tell the difference between the two pie pans. Add 1 tablespoon of table salt to the second pie pan and spread the salt evenly over the bottom of the pan by gently shaking it as you did the first pan.

Using an oven mitt, place the aluminum pie pans in the hot oven and close the oven door. After 1 minute, carefully check the contents of the two pans. One of the solids should have started to melt. Continue heating until this solid melts completely. This should take only a few minutes.

Turn off the oven, and use an oven mitt to remove the alu-

FIGURE A: Salt and sugar before heating in an oven

minum pan containing the melted solid from the oven. Tilt the pan and observe how the melted solid flows as a liquid. Place this pan on a hot pad. Next, remove the aluminum pan left in the oven and place this pan also on a hot pad. **Do not touch the pans or the material in the pans because they are hot.**

Use a measuring spoon to probe the molten liquid. Be careful not to burn yourself. Note how long it takes for it to resolidify.

Carefully feel the bottom of both aluminum pans after they have cooled for 10 minutes. If the pans are cool enough to touch, hold the aluminum pie pan containing the solid that was melted with both hands. Bend the pie pan in the middle. What happens?

You should find in this experiment that the table sugar melts and the table salt remains a solid when both are heated in an oven set to 450°F (232°C). You may also observe that the sugar turns slightly brown as it melts. The brown color is caused by oxygen in the air changing some of the melted sugar into new substances. You should also observe that the melted sugar turns back to a solid, in the form of a sheet, soon after it is allowed to cool.

Table sugar and table salt are examples of pure solids. Pure solids contain particles that are packed very closely together in a regular way. There is very little space between the particles that make up the solid.

In crystals of table sugar, molecules called *sucrose* are the particles that are packed closely together. In crystals of table salt, ions are the particles that are packed closely together. Ions are atoms that have a charge that is either positive or negative. Table salt, which is also called *sodium chloride*, is made up of positive sodium ions and negative chlorine ions. The sodium ions have a positive charge, and the chlorine ions have a negative charge.

When a solid melts, it changes into a liquid. Heat energy is necessary for a solid to melt. During the melting process, the particles that make up the solid become free to move around.

Pure solids usually melt at a definite temperature. The temperature at which a pure solid melts is called the *melting point* of the solid. Table sugar has a melting point of 367°F (186°C), while the melting point of table salt is much higher at 1474°F (801°C).

In this experiment only the table sugar melts. This is because the temperature of the oven, which is set to 450°F (232°C), is greater than the melting point of the table sugar. The oven provides enough heat energy for the sugar to melt. The temperature of the oven is much lower than the melting point of table salt, however. This is why the table salt did not melt. In fact, table salt cannot be melted in an ordinary kitchen oven because the maximum temperature of a kitchen oven is around 550°F (288°C). Because table salt has such a high melting point, it can only be melted in special ovens.

Table salt has a higher melting point than table sugar because it takes more heat energy to move apart the sodium ions and chlorine ions that make up table salt than it does to move apart the sucrose molecules in solid table sugar. The attraction between sodium and chlorine ions is greater than the attraction between the individual sugar molecules in table sugar. Generally, solids that are made up of ions have high melting points because oppositely charged ions have strong attractions for each other. Can you think of other solids that are made of ions?

CHANGING SUGAR TO CARBON

MATERIALS NEEDED

Oven

Watch or clock

Measuring cup

Table sugar

Aluminum pie pan

Oven mitt

Fork

❗ **Alert! Adult supervision needed.**

What is sugar? Is there a way to change sugar into a substance that is mostly carbon? In this experiment you will learn how one substance can be changed into another and how carbon fibers are made and used.

Turn the oven temperature to 450°F (232°C), and wait 12 minutes until the oven is hot. Pour ⅓ cup (80 ml) of table sugar into the middle of an aluminum pie pan. Using an oven mitt, place the pie pan on a rack in the oven, as shown in Figure A. Close the oven door, and wait while the sugar becomes hot. If you have an exhaust fan above your oven, turn it on. There may be a small amount of smoke as the sugar is heated.

After 10 minutes, open the oven door and observe the sugar in the pan. Close the door and, after 10 minutes, open the door and observe the sugar again. Once again, close the oven and wait 10 minutes. The sugar has now been in the oven for a total of 30 minutes. Turn off the oven and use an oven mitt to remove the pie pan from the oven. Place the pie pan on top of the stove to cool.

While the pie pan is still warm, place a fork in the dark substance in the pan and slowly pull out the fork, as shown in Figure B. What do you observe? Wait about 30 minutes, and once again observe the substance in the pie pan.

You should observe that the white crystals of sugar are changed to a black powder. You may observe that the white sugar initially melts and forms a reddish brown liquid. Bubbles form in the liquid and the liquid turns a darker color. Finally, after 30 minutes, you should observe that the white sugar is completely gone and the pan is filled with a puffy, black solid. You may hear a cracking sound as the spaces trapped in the solid break and the solid collapses to a flat shape.

FIGURE B

When you put a fork into the pan, you may be able to pull out a long string of black material, as shown in Figure B. After you pull out this long, sticky liquid, it dries and forms a long, thin, reddish black string.

In this experiment, sugar is changed by heating from one substance to another. Sugar is made of molecules that contain carbon, hydrogen, and oxygen atoms. When the sugar is heated, molecules of water are driven off from the sugar and the sugar is changed to a new substance. Caramel, a type of flavoring used in candy, is made by heating sugar. If caramel is cooked too long, it can turn black.

At 450°F (232°C) water coming from the sugar exists as a gas called *steam*. As steam forms in the sugar, it forms bubbles that expand in the liquid. The steam makes the remaining liquid expand to take up more space. When the liquid cools and hardens to a solid, it is light and puffy. As the spaces in the solid break, the sticky solid may collapse to form a flat, hard solid. You can break this solid up into small flakes of black powder.

This powder is mostly carbon with some hydrogen and oxygen atoms and looks like charcoal. Charcoal is made by heating wood in the absence of oxygen. Wood charcoal is used as a fuel for small cooking fires and is also used in making gunpowder.

Coal is a natural fuel that is formed from forest matter trapped and heated underground for millions of years.

The long string of black material you pull out of the pan is carbon, somewhat like the carbon fibers used to make many modern materials. Carbon fibers are made by *pyrolysis*, a chemical change brought about by heat. In this industrial process, a fiber that includes carbon atoms as part of its structure, such as natural wool or synthetic polyacrylonitrile (PAN), is used. Bundles of the starting fibers (thousands of filaments) are heated in a furnace in an atmosphere with an inert gas such as argon but with no oxygen. During heating, gases—such as water, carbon dioxide, and ammonia—are given off. In a final heat treatment that may be as high as 5600°F (3093°C), extremely strong and tough graphite filaments are produced. Pure carbon melts at a temperature of more than 6400°F (3538°C).

These special carbon fibers are used for constructing parts for modern boats and airplanes and even rocket ships. The Delta Clipper-Experimental (DC-X) rocket is made of a mixture of epoxy and graphite fibers called a *composite material*. The outer surface of the rocket is only about as thick as a credit card. Because the rocket is much lighter than the usual aluminum construction, it is able to take off and land. The DC-X is the first rocket that can be completely used over and over again.

4

FORMING CRYSTALS

MATTER

MATERIALS NEEDED

Measuring cup

Water

Drinking glass

Measuring spoons

Teaspoon

Table salt

Black construction
  paper

Plate

Have you ever wondered how salt crystals are formed? Why do all the crystals of salt in a salt shaker seem to be the same size and shape? In this experiment you will try to make crystals of salt from salt and learn the answers to these questions.

Pour 1 cup (0.24 l) of hot tap water into a large drinking glass. Add 4 teaspoons (20 ml) of table salt to this glass. Stir the salt water until all the salt dissolves. When the salt dissolves, it will seem to disappear.

Put a piece of black construction paper on a plate. Pour a teaspoon (5 ml) of salt water on the construction paper to make one big drop about 1.2 inches (3 cm) across. You may want to make several of these drops on the construction paper. Set the plate with the construction paper where it will not be disturbed for a day. Observe the drop(s) of water on the construction paper several hours later, and then observe again the next day.

After several hours, or by the next day, you should see small white crystals form on the black paper, as shown in Figure A. As

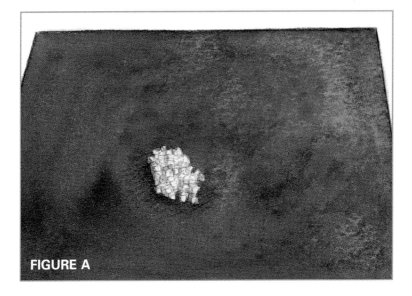

FIGURE A

time passes, the water evaporates (goes into the air), but the salt is left behind to form crystals. Each crystal should have a cubic shape—like a box. As you look down on the crystals, they should look similar in shape to the crystals of salt you might pour out of a salt shaker. However, you may find that the crystals on the black paper are larger in size than salt-shaker crystals.

Table salt is called sodium chloride because it is made of positive atoms of sodium and negative atoms of chlorine. These positive and negative atoms are called *ions*. In sodium chloride the ions combine in equal amounts of positive and negative so there is no excess charge in the salt.

When you dissolve the table salt in water, sodium ions and chlorine ions spread throughout the water and the salt seems to disappear. However, as the water evaporates, the liquid becomes more concentrated salt water, and the ions move closer together. Since opposite charges attract, the negative chlorine ions are attracted to the positive sodium ions. The ions combine to re-form a solid salt made of a mixture of sodium and chlorine ions. These ions combine to form a cube-shaped crystal, as shown in Figure B.

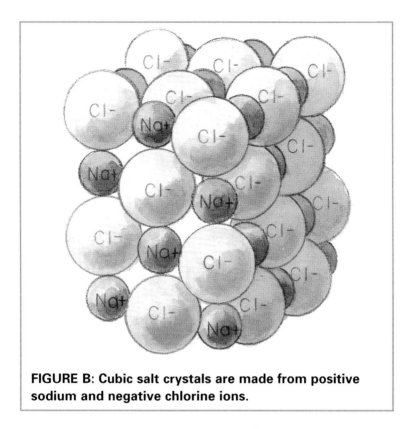

FIGURE B: Cubic salt crystals are made from positive sodium and negative chlorine ions.

There are many places around the world, including the United States, Canada, Mexico, and Europe, where pure deposits of salt can be found. These deposits of rock salt were formed by the evaporation of seawater millions of years ago. As the water evaporated, salt was left behind. The pure sodium chloride (NaCl) found in nature is a mineral called *halite*. This salt can be mined, leaving underground rooms supported by pillars of salt.

Another way to produce salt is to evaporate seawater and collect the salt that remains behind. The heat from the sun is used to evaporate the water. Concentrated salt water called *brine* forms in large open ponds. This concentrated salt water is then run through pans, where crystals of solid salt are formed and collected. Can you think of other ways you could form and collect salt?

5

MAKING A SOLID FROM IONS IN SOLUTION

MATTER

MATERIALS NEEDED

Felt pen

Masking tape

Small glass jar with lid

Ruler

Measuring cup

Safety goggles (available in hardware stores)

Ammonia, clear type

Use ammonia with care, read caution on label.

Tablespoon

Epsom salt

Water

Large glass

Clock or watch

! Alert! Adult supervision needed.

In this experiment, you will try to change a solution of ions into a solid.

Caution—Ammonia can be harmful if not used properly. Do not allow ammonia to get on your skin or in your eyes. Ammonia is a basic (alkaline) liquid. Do not mix ammonia with liquids other than water. Return ammonia to a safe location away from young children when finished. Use safety goggles for eye protection when pouring the ammonia.

Write *ammonia* on a piece of tape, and put this tape on the small glass jar. Put on your safety goggles. Add enough clear ammonia to cover the bottom of this jar to a depth of about 0.75 in. (2 cm).

Add 2 tablespoons (30 ml) of Epsom salt to 1 cup (0.24 l) of room-temperature water in a large glass. Epsom salt is available in drugstores or in the pharmacy section of large grocery stores. Stir until all the Epsom salt dissolves and the water is again clear and colorless (not cloudy).

Add 2 tablespoons (30 ml) of the clear Epsom salt (magnesium sulfate) solution to the jar of ammonia, as shown in Figure A. What happens when these two clear liquids are added together? Cover the jar with a lid, and put it in a safe place for 1 hour. After an hour, observe the jar again. What has happened?

Pour the liquid from the jar down the drain and rinse the jar with large amounts of water to remove all the ammonia.

When you mix the solution of Epsom salt and ammonia

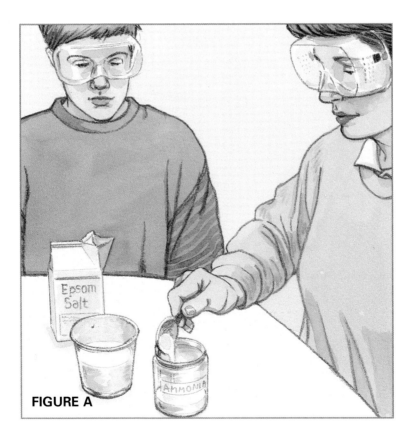

FIGURE A

together, you probably observe that the mixture turns white. Tiny solid particles form, and this gives the mixture a cloudy white appearance. After the jar sets for an hour, you should see that these white solid particles settle to the bottom of the jar. This white solid comes from a combination of some of the positive and negative ions found in your mixture of ammonia and Epsom salt solutions.

The white solid that forms is called *magnesium hydroxide*. It is made from a combination of magnesium ions (Mg^{+2}) and hydroxide ions (OH^{-1}). A magnesium ion is a magnesium atom that has a +2 charge. A hydroxide ion is a hydrogen atom and an oxygen atom that are held together and have a -1 charge. If both these ions are present in sufficient amounts in water, they will combine to form the *ionic* (made of ions) solid magnesium hydroxide.

In your experiment, ammonia is the source of the hydroxide ions. Ammonia (NH_3) is a base, and when it is dissolved in water (H_2O), it produces ammonium (NH_4^+) and hydroxide (OH^-) ions. The hydroxide ions in the ammonia solution and the magnesium ions in the Epsom salt solution come together when these liquids are mixed together. Ions of magnesium and hydroxide combine to form the solid called magnesium hydroxide.

Chemists write magnesium hydroxide as $Mg(OH)_2$ to show that there are 2 hydroxide ions for every 1 magnesium ion. An ionic solid is always some combination of positive and negative ions. There are thousands of different kinds of ionic solids. For example, table salt is a kind of ionic solid. Table salt is called sodium chloride because it is made up of positive sodium ions and negative chlorine ions.

Every 1000 lb (453 kg) of seawater contains about 1.3 lb (0.6 kg) of magnesium ions, 19 lb (8.6 kg) of chlorine ions, 11 lb (5 kg) of sodium ions, and smaller amounts of many other ions. Magnesium metal is produced from the magnesium ions found in seawater. In Freeport, Texas, there is a large facility for obtaining magnesium from seawater.

When lime (calcium oxide) is added to water, hydroxide ions are produced. When lime is added to seawater, the magnesium in the seawater combines with the hydroxide to form the white solid magnesium hydroxide.

To complete the conversion of seawater to magnesium metal, the solid magnesium hydroxide is separated from the remaining liquid. Next, a special acid, hydrochloric acid, is added to the solid. A strong electric current is then passed through this solution, forming magnesium metal along with chlorine gas.

It is interesting that the lime used in this process comes from something found in the sea. Shells dragged up from the bottom of the ocean are made of a mineral called *calcium carbonate*. When these calcium carbonate shells are heated to a high temperature, carbon dioxide gas is given off, and lime (calcium oxide) is formed. Can you think of other products that come from the sea?

6

TEMPERATURE CHANGES WITH SALT IN WATER

| MATTER | HEAT | ENERGY |

MATERIALS NEEDED

Two measuring cups

Epsom salt

Water

Large plastic glass

Thermometer (out-
door type)

Spoon

In this experiment, you will add Epsom salt to water and measure any temperature change that occurs.

Use a measuring cup to measure ½ cup (120 ml) of Epsom salt. Epsom salt is available in drugstores or in the pharmacy section of large grocery stores.

Read the label on the Epsom salt box. Do not taste the Epsom salt or drink the Epsom salt water you prepare.

Use the other measuring cup to pour ½ cup of water into a large plastic glass. Use water that is room temperature. Place an outdoor thermometer in the water. Wait about 10 minutes to allow time for the water and the solid Epsom salt to come to room temperature. Use the thermometer to read the temperature of the water.

Remove the thermometer from the glass, and add the entire ½ cup of Epsom salt to the glass of water. Stir the water and Epsom salt together with a spoon for about 20 seconds. Then place the thermometer back into the glass with the Epsom salt and water, as shown in Figure A. Observe the temperature on the ther-

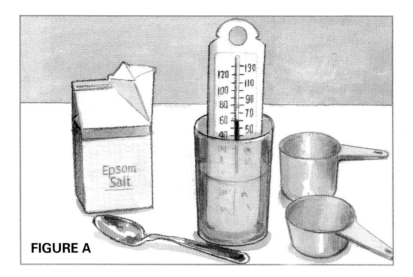

FIGURE A

mometer. Is the temperature the same as before? If the temperature has changed, how many degrees different is it from the temperature before the salt was added? Feel the outside of the glass. How does it feel?

You should observe that the temperature decreases after the Epsom salt is added to water. You may find a decrease of 14°F (8°C) or more.

Epsom salt is made of many positive magnesium ions and negative sulfate ions. Each magnesium ion is a charged (+2) magnesium atom. Each sulfate ion is a charged (-2) collection of 1 sulfur atom and 4 oxygen atoms. Epsom salt is called a *hydrated salt* because it also includes water molecules as part of the solid. There can be up to 7 water molecules for each magnesium and sulfate ion.

When Epsom salt is placed in water, the positive magnesium ions and negative sulfate ions can separate from each other and spread into the water. The water molecules that are part of the salt are released and become part of the molecules of water in the salt-water solution.

It takes energy to separate the ions and water molecules in Epsom salt from one another. However, energy is released when these ions are surrounded by water molecules. If more energy is released than is used, heat is given off, and the process is called *exothermic*. If more energy is used than is released, heat is taken in, and the process is called *endothermic*. An exothermic change feels hot. An endothermic change feels cold. Was the temperature change you measured exothermic or endothermic?

Exothermic changes may be more familiar to you than endothermic ones. Combustion is a familiar exothermic reaction. When wood is burned, it gets hot and gives off heat because it is an exothermic reaction. Energy stored in the *bonds* (connections between atoms) is released when the atoms are rearranged into new molecules. Carbon atoms in burning wood combine with oxygen in the air to form carbon dioxide and release heat.

Cold packs and hot packs are interesting uses of salts to cause temperature changes. Ammonium nitrate is a salt that causes an endothermic change when added to water. Calcium chloride is a salt that causes an exothermic change when added to water. You should never open cold or hot packs or try to remove the salt from these packs.

A cold pack consists of a container of the white ammonium nitrate solid separated from water. When the separation between the white solid and water is broken by squeezing or bending the cold pack, the ammonium nitrate dissolves in the water, and the pack gets cold. These cold packs are often used to treat sprains or other injuries because cold helps reduce swelling.

A hot pack may contain the salt calcium chloride. When the separation between calcium chloride and water is broken by squeezing or bending the hot pack, the calcium chloride dissolves in water and the pack gets warm. These hot packs are sometimes used as a small heat supply for someone who is outdoors in the winter. They are also used to help increase blood supply to a local area of the body to speed the healing process. Can you think of other uses for processes that get cold or hot?

7

A SALT
THAT HOLDS
WATER

HEAT   MATTER   ENERGY

MATERIALS NEEDED

Measuring cup

Epsom salt

Aluminum pie pan

Oven

Clock

Spoon

Oven mitt

Large glass jar with lid

Thermometer (out-
door type)

Drinking glass

Water

Magnifying lens

! **Alert! Adult supervision needed.**

In this experiment, you will measure the temperature change that occurs when water is added to Epsom salt that has been dried in an oven.

Add ½ cup (120 ml) of Epsom salt to an aluminum pie pan. Epsom salt is available in drugstores or in the pharmacy section of large grocery stores. **Read the label on the Epsom salt. Do not taste the Epsom salt or drink the Epsom salt water you prepare.**

Spread the Epsom salt until the bottom of the pie pan is covered. Place the pie pan on a rack in the oven. Close the oven door, and turn the temperature setting to 400°F (204°C). Heat the Epsom salt in the oven for 1 hour at 400°F.

After 1 hour turn off the oven, and use an oven mitt to remove the pie pan. Set the pie pan on the stove top and allow it to cool for 10 minutes. Use a spoon to place the dried Epsom salt into a large glass jar, and screw a lid on the jar. The salt may stick together in a clump and may need to be broken apart with the spoon. Wait 40 minutes to be sure the Epsom salt in the jar has cooled to the temperature of the room.

Place a thermometer into the Epsom salt in the jar. Observe the temperature of the Epsom salt.

Remove the thermometer from the jar, and measure the temperature of a glass of water. Use water that is neither hot nor cold but the same temperature as the room. Add ¼ cup (60 ml) of this water to the Epsom salt in the jar. Use a spoon to stir the water and Epsom salt together for about 20 seconds. The mixture may now look like a thick, wet paste. Now place the thermometer back into the jar with the Epsom salt and water. Observe the temperature on the thermometer. Cautiously feel the outside of the glass. How does it feel?

You should see a large increase in temperature after the water is added to the Epsom salt. The temperature may increase by 40°F (22°C) or more.

Epsom salt is found as a naturally occurring mineral called *epsomite*. Epsomite, or Epsom salt, is made of magnesium sulfate and attached water molecules. A salt that includes water molecules as part of the solid is a hydrated salt. The waters are trapped in the solid, and the salt looks and feels dry. However, when a hydrated salt is heated, the waters of hydration can be driven off or removed from the salt. A salt which has had this water removed is called an *anhydrous salt*.

It takes energy to separate the salt and its molecules of water. When the hydrated Epsom salt is heated in the oven, energy is used to drive off the water. However, energy is released when these molecules of water become reattached to the anhydrous (dried) salt. When you added water to the Epsom salt in the jar, the water molecules attach to the salt and energy is released. The mixture becomes extremely hot, and you should see a significant increase in the temperature of the salt and water mixture.

An ion is a charged atom or charged group of atoms. Epsom salt is made of magnesium ions (+2 charge) and sulfate ions (-2 charge). There can be up to 7 molecules of water for each magnesium and sulfate ion. These water molecules differ in how hard they are to remove by heating. For example, the first 4 water molecules can be removed by heating to 176°F (80°C), the fifth by heating to 212°F (100°C), the sixth by heating to 248°F (120°C). However, Epsom salt does not lose the seventh and last molecule of water until the temperature is raised to 482°F (250°C).

Since you heated the salt to 400°F, how many water molecules did you remove? You should have driven off 6 of the 7 water molecules surrounding each magnesium sulfate. The form of magnesium sulfate with only 1 molecule of water is found in a natural mineral called *kieserite*. When you heat the original Epsom salt (epsomite) to form kieserite, you may notice that the original hydrated salt (epsomite) has a crystalline appearance while the dried, anhydrous salt (kieserite) is more like a powder. Examine both forms of Epsom salt with a magnifying lens. How would you describe the difference in their appearance?

Many useful salts and minerals are found in naturally occurring deposits and are mined directly. Other salts and solids can be changed through some chemical process such as heating. In this experiment, you converted the mineral epsomite to kieserite by heating. You can see how different the properties of these two minerals are by adding water to each of them.

COOL TO THE TOUCH

MATERIALS NEEDED

Heavy metal cooking pot

Styrofoam cup

Have you ever touched different solid objects in a room that were all the temperature of the room and found that some of the objects felt cooler than others? In this experiment you will use your sense of touch to explore heat flow and the heat capacities of two different solid objects.

For this experiment you will need to make sure that the metal cooking pot and the styrofoam cup are at the same temperature. To do this, place both objects on the same table or countertop and leave them there for 1 hour. This will allow the pot and cup to reach room temperature if they are not already at this temperature. Room temperature varies with season and location, but a typical range is 65° to 80°F (18° to 27°C).

Hold the styrofoam cup in your hands for 15 seconds. Then touch and hold the sides of the metal pot with your hands. Which object feels cooler to the touch?

Although the styrofoam cup and the metal pot are the same temperature, the metal pot will feel much cooler to the touch than the styrofoam cup.

The temperature of your hand is around body temperature, which is 98.6°F (37°C). Both the styrofoam cup and the metal pot are at room temperature. When you touch the cup or the pot, heat flows out of your hand and into whichever object you are holding. Heat flows out of your hand because your hand is warmer than either the styrofoam cup or the metal pot. Heat always flows from a warmer object to a cooler object.

Heat moves out of your hand quickly when you touch the metal pot because metal is a good conductor of heat. Styrofoam is a poor conductor of heat, so heat moves out of your hand more slowly when you hold the styrofoam cup. A metal pot also holds more heat than a styrofoam cup. A metal pot has a larger capacity, or ability, to absorb and hold heat. Because the metal pot absorbs more heat and absorbs heat more quickly from your hand, the metal pot feels cooler to the touch than does the styrofoam cup.

What would you feel if the metal pot is warmer than your hand when you touched it?

Different objects have different capacities to absorb and hold heat. Generally, objects that contain lots of material, or mass, have large capacities to hold heat. Objects at room temperature that have large capacities to hold heat and are also good conductors of heat will feel cool to the touch. Some examples are objects made of marble, metal, and stone.

Materials with large capacities to absorb and hold heat are used in building solar homes. For example, it is common to put down thick slate or tile floors in rooms receiving large amounts of sunlight. Some of the light striking the floor is changed into heat, which is then absorbed by the floor. Thick slate or tile floors hold large amounts of heat, heat which is then slowly released into the room during the night. It is also common to build a thick wall out of stone or brick in a room that receives lots of sunlight. The wall heats up when the sun strikes it, and because stone and brick have a large capacity to hold heat, much of the sun's heat is stored in the wall for long periods of time. Can you think of other uses for solid materials with large heat capacities?

9

CHANGING A POWDER INTO A HARD SOLID

MATTER   HEAT

MATERIALS NEEDED

Measuring cup

Water

Plaster of Paris
(available at most
hardware and craft
stores)

Clock

Plastic spoon

Aluminum pie pan

Paper cup

Can a powder be changed into a hard solid? In this experiment you will examine this possibility.

The directions given in the next paragraph for mixing plaster of Paris are the directions described on most containers of plaster of Paris. Read the mixing directions on your container of plaster of Paris. Follow the mixing directions on your container if they are different from the directions described in the next paragraph.

Pour ¼ cup (60 ml) of water into a paper cup. Without stirring, slowly sprinkle ½ cup (120 ml) of plaster of Paris into the water, as shown in Figure A. After 5 minutes, stir the water and plaster of Paris mixture with a plastic spoon until it forms a thick, smooth paste. Feel the outside surface of the paper cup. How does it feel?

Pour the thick plaster of Paris mixture into an aluminum pie pan, as shown in Figure B. The paste will form a puddle in the pie

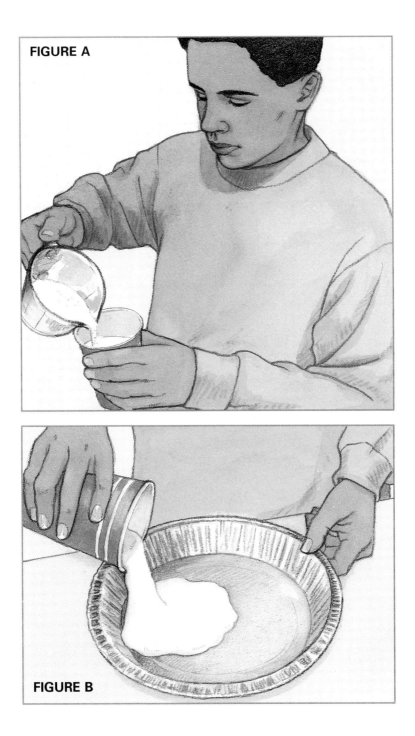

FIGURE A

FIGURE B

pan, but the puddle probably will not completely fill the bottom of the pan. Do not disturb the puddle for 1 hour. After 1 hour, touch the puddle. Has the mixture of plaster of Paris changed?

You should find that it has changed from a paste to a hard solid. Allow the plaster of Paris to dry for 24 hours.

Plaster of Paris, also simply known as *plaster*, is made from gypsum. Gypsum is a white, chalky mineral that is mined from the earth. Major gypsum deposits in the United States are found in New York and Michigan, but some of the earliest gypsum mines were found outside Paris, France. This is how plaster of Paris got its name.

Gypsum consists of two tightly combined chemical substances. These two substances are calcium sulfate and water. When gypsum is heated, some of the water that is combined with the calcium sulfate is removed from the solid and evaporates away. Plaster of Paris is produced when just the right amount of water is removed from gypsum.

Plaster of Paris is ground to a fine powder before it is packaged and sold. When mixed with water, the powder immediately combines with the water to re-form gypsum. As the gypsum re-forms, heat is produced. You feel this heat when you touch the outside surface of the paper cup you used to mix water with your plaster of Paris.

The gypsum that re-forms when water and plaster of Paris combine is made of tiny crystals that look like fibers. The thick, pasty plaster becomes solid and hard when these fiberlike crystals of gypsum interlock with one another. Also, as the gypsum crystals interlock, the plaster expands slightly. This is why plaster is particularly useful in filling cracks and molds.

Cement, an important building material, is another powder that forms a solid when mixed with water. Unlike plaster of Paris, cement forms an extremely strong, stonelike solid when mixed with water. Like plaster, cement hardens by forming interlocking crystals.

Cement is made by heating ground limestone, sand, and

clay together at a high temperature. The world production of cement is over 1500 billion lb (680 billion kg) with most of this production going into the making of concrete. Concrete, which is made by mixing water with cement, is used to construct many roads, bridges, sidewalks, and buildings. Can you identify objects made from concrete near where you live?

WATER-ABSORBING SOLID

MATTER

MATERIALS NEEDED

Aluminum pie pan

Table salt

Have you ever noticed that table salt usually pours more slowly from a salt shaker when the air is humid, such as after it has rained for several days? In this experiment you will learn why.

On a humid day, sprinkle table salt into an aluminum pie pan until the bottom of the pan is covered with the salt, as shown in Figure A. Gently shake the pan sideways and notice how the salt moves freely in the pan.

Place the pan of table salt outside. If it is raining, make sure the pan is in a spot that is sheltered from the rain, such as on a covered porch. Check the pan of table salt after 1 hour by gently shaking it sideways. Continue to check the pan each hour for several more hours.

After an hour or so, you should find that the salt does not move freely when you shake the pan sideways. Instead, you may find that much of the salt has clumped together. After several hours you may find puddles of water scattered around the pan, and it may appear that some of the salt has disappeared.

Table salt and water have a strong attraction for each other. It is this strong attraction between water and table salt that explains why table salt dissolves in water. Also because of this strong attraction, table salt can absorb water from humid air.

FIGURE A

When table salt absorbs water from the air, the individual salt crystals begin to stick together. This is why the salt in the pan does not move freely when you shake the pan sideways after it has been outside for an hour or so. This is also why table salt pours more slowly from a salt shaker on a rainy or humid day.

When table salt is left in humid air for several hours, the salt may absorb so much water that puddles appear. These puddles are not pure water but puddles of salt water. When table salt absorbs large amounts of water, the salt dissolves in the water that is absorbed. This is how the puddles form. If table salt is left in humid air long enough, the salt may absorb so much water that all the salt dissolves in the water that was absorbed and only puddles of salt water remain.

Substances that can absorb water from the air are called *hygroscopic substances.* In addition to table salt, other hygroscopic substances often found in a kitchen are flour, rice, sugar, and popcorn that has been popped. Can you think of other water-absorbing substances?

Many hardware stores sell a product that can be used around the house to remove water from the air in small spaces such as closets and cabinets. This keeps the closets and cabinets from smelling musty or developing mildew. The product is an airtight container holding pellets of solid *calcium chloride*, a hygroscopic salt that readily absorbs large amounts of water from the air. When the product is to be used, the lid of the container is lifted and the container is placed in a closed space where the moisture in the air is high, such as a damp closet or cabinet.

Silica gel is a hygroscopic solid often packaged with electronic equipment, such as cameras and calculators, to keep the equipment dry during shipment and storage before it is purchased. The silica gel is usually contained in a small white pouch about the size of a quarter. Can you think of other ways to use a water-absorbing material?

11

COLOR-ADSORBING CARBON

MATTER

MATERIALS NEEDED

Sharp pencil

Paper cup

Water

Two coffee filters (the type used in auto-matic coffee makers)

Activated carbon (used in aquarium filters, found in stores selling pet supplies)

Two bowls

Measuring cup

Can of purple grape soda

What color is grape soda? Do you think you could change grape soda to a colorless liquid that you could see through? In this experiment you will explore the ability of *granules* (small pieces) of activated carbon to adsorb or trap molecules on its surface.

Use a sharp pencil to poke a small hole, about ⅛ in. (3 mm) across, in the bottom of a paper cup. Fill the bottom of the paper cup with water and make sure the water drains out in a thin stream. If the water only drips out, then you need to make the hole slightly larger.

Place two coffee filters together, and push them down inside the paper cup. The filters should line the inside of the paper cup. Then add enough acti-vated carbon to completely fill the inside of the paper cup. It should take between ½ (120 ml) and 1 cup (0.24 l) of carbon to fill the paper cup. The carbon will be inside the filters, which will keep extremely small carbon particles from passing out of the cup.

Hold the paper cup above the first bowl, and slowly pour ½ cup (120 ml) of water onto the carbon in the paper cup. Allow the water to drip through the carbon, through the filters, and into the bowl. If the water does not seem to be draining out of the cup, lift the coffee filter slightly higher in the cup and the water should go out faster.

After a few minutes, when all the water has drained through, hold the paper cup over a second clean bowl. Slowly pour ½ cup of purple grape soda into the carbon in the paper cup, as shown in Figure A. Allow the purple grape soda to drip through the carbon and into the bowl.

What color is the grape soda that collects in the bowl?

You should observe that the purple grape soda loses most or all of its color as it passes through the activated carbon particles. You may observe that the grape soda passing through the carbon

FIGURE A

has a faint bluish color. The purple color of grape soda is a mixture of red and blue dye molecules. If the red dye is removed more easily than the blue dye, it will leave the grape soda with a bluish color. If the grape soda that collects in the bowl still contains some color, try pouring the soda again through the carbon granules in the paper cup.

In this experiment the molecules that give grape soda its characteristic color are removed through adsorption. When molecules from a gas or liquid stick on the surface of a solid, like carbon, the process is called *adsorption*. Some but not all of the molecules are adsorbed. In the grape soda the molecules of water and the molecules of sugar are not adsorbed. However, the molecules that give grape soda its color are adsorbed by the activated carbon powder.

Activated carbon powder is formed when carbon reacts with steam at a high temperature, such as 1000°F (538°C). The steam removes parts of the carbon so that the surface becomes much rougher and becomes filled with holes called *pores*. Carbon that has been activated contains a large surface area.

To understand how small pieces of carbon could have a large surface area, imagine a piece of newspaper crumpled up into a tiny ball. This tiny wad of newspaper may not seem very big. However, if you unfold it and spread it out, it would seem to have a much larger surface area. In the same way, tiny pieces of carbon can have a very large surface area.

The large surface area of activated carbon makes it extremely effective in removing or trapping molecules of gas or liquid on its surface. Activated carbon is used in filters to purify drinking water or the water used in aquariums. Activated carbon traps or adsorbs molecules found in the water just like it traps dye molecules in your grape soda.

Activated carbon is also used in filters to help purify air by removing odors or pollutant molecules from the air. Gas masks containing activated carbon have been used by soldiers to remove poisonous gases from the air they breathe. The air passes through a carbon filter in the mask. Nitrogen molecules and oxygen molecules pass through the filter without being trapped. However, any poisonous molecules that may be released into the air by enemy soldiers are adsorbed by the activated carbon in the filter. Gas masks were used widely in World War I but have been used rarely in other wars as countries have tried to outlaw the use of chemical weapons.

12

LIGHT FROM A SOLID

MATERIALS NEEDED

Wintergreen-flavored hard candy (such as Certs, Life Savers, or Tic Tac)

Plastic food wrap

Pliers

Dark room

There are many ways in which light is made. The most common way is to pass electricity through a lightbulb. The lightbulb changes electric energy into light energy. Light is also made by burning materials such as candles and wood. Do you think that light can be made by crushing a solid? In this experiment you will find out.

Place a wintergreen-flavored hard candy on a piece of plastic wrap. The hard candy must contain sugar, so do not use sugar-free candy. Fold the plastic wrap over the hard candy several times. Grasp and hold the wrapped hard candy in a pair of pliers, as seen in Figure A. Do not squeeze the pliers just yet.

Take the pliers holding the hard candy into a dark room, such as a closet. You may want to do this experiment at night so that the room will be as dark as possible. Once you are in the dark room, wait 1 minute to allow your eyes to adjust to the darkness. Now, while looking at the pliers, slowly squeeze them so as to crush the hard candy. What do you observe?

As you slowly crush the hard candy, you should see tiny, bright flashes of bluish-colored light coming from the candy.

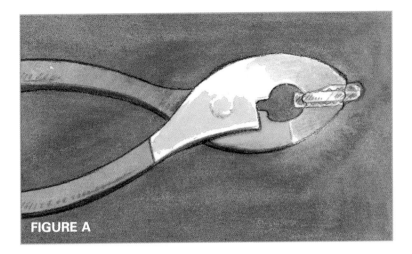

These sparks of light are due to a complex series of events that take place when the wintergreen-flavored hard candy is crushed.

In the first step of the light-making process, sugar crystals in the hard candy are made to crack by the crushing action of the pliers. As a sugar crystal starts to crack, a positive charge develops on one side of the crack and a negative charge develops on the other side. When the crack in the sugar crystal becomes large enough, electrons jump from the negative side to the positive side of the crack, like miniature bolts of lightning. A bolt of lightning between the ground and clouds is caused by the explosive movement of electrons between ground that is negatively charged and clouds that are positively charged.

As the electrons jump from the negative side to the positive side of the cracking sugar crystal, they collide with air molecules that are present in the crack. The air molecules absorb some of the energy from the quickly moving electrons. This causes the air molecules to become excited and to produce ultraviolet light. We cannot see ultraviolet light because our eyes are not sensitive to it. It is the ultraviolet light from the sun that causes us to tan, and, in the case of too much exposure, to burn.

The ultraviolet light given off by the excited air molecules is captured by the wintergreen molecules present in the wintergreen-flavored candy. The wintergreen molecules in turn become excited, or take on extra energy, when they capture this ultraviolet light. After becoming excited, they quickly give off visible light that is bluish in color. This is the light you observed when you crushed your wintergreen-flavored hard candy.

Repeat this experiment with wintergreen-flavored hard candy that is sugar-free. Do you see any light flashes from the sugar-free candy?

During an earthquake, rocks in the ground and along earthquake fissures experience tremendous pressures that can cause the rock to shatter into a powder. When this occurs, light is often produced in a process similar to that observed in this experiment. Miners have also observed flashes of light coming from rock while working in deep underground mines. These flashes of light are feared because they can mean a rock collapse is about to happen.

13

SOUND-ABSORBING AND SOUND-REFLECTING SOLIDS

MATERIALS NEEDED

Empty room without carpeting (such as a basement or garage)

Furnished room with carpeting

Have you ever walked into a crowded room where everyone seemed to be talking, and yet the room seemed quiet? Or have you ever walked into a room that seemed unusually noisy? In this experiment you will study solid objects that can either absorb or reflect sound.

For this experiment you will compare the loudness of a clapping sound made in an empty room and made in a carpeted room filled with furniture. To begin the experiment, find an empty room without carpeting and little, if any, furniture. A basement, garage, or even a bathroom should work well. If you are at school, an empty gymnasium should work. Go to the center of the empty room, and listen carefully as you clap your hands several times.

Then, go into a room that contains furniture and has carpeting on the floor. Again, listen carefully as you clap your hands several times while standing in the center of the room. What differences do you hear?

You should find that the clapping sound is louder and seems to last longer in the empty room. You may even hear a slight echo when you clap in the empty room. However, in the

FIGURE A: Comparing clapping sounds in an empty room and a room filled with furniture

carpeted room filled with furniture, the clapping sound may seem muffled or dull.

Sound is a form of energy—just like heat, light, and electricity. Sound energy travels in waves similar to the waves that spread out when a stone is dropped in a pool, puddle, or sink of water.

Sound waves are created by the motion of a vibrating object. For example, when a musical drum is struck, the covering of the drum vibrates. The vibrating causes air molecules around the drum to vibrate, and this starts a sound wave. The vibrating air molecules near the drum cause neighboring air molecules surrounding them to start vibrating. These newly vibrating air molecules cause air molecules surrounding them to start vibrating; this, in turn, causes air molecules surrounding them to start vibrating; and so on. The vibration of air molecules rapidly spreads across the room.

Sound waves can either bounce off or be absorbed by solid objects. If the solid object is hard and smooth, like a ceiling or wall, the sound waves tend to bounce off, or be reflected by, the solid object. When you clap your hands in the empty room, sound waves can be reflected many times from the walls, ceiling, and floor before all the energy in the sound waves is finally absorbed. This is why your clapping sound should seem loud and also seem to last a while after you stop clapping. Echoes are often heard in empty rooms, and empty rooms often seem loud.

Instead of being reflected, sound waves are absorbed by objects that are spongy and soft, like fabric-covered furniture, drapes, and carpeting. Sound waves can penetrate into spongy and soft objects. When a sound wave penetrates a spongy and soft object, the energy of the sound wave is quickly absorbed by the object. This is why, when you clap your hands in the carpeted room with furniture, the clapping sound seems muffled and dull. The sound waves from your clapping are absorbed by the carpeting and furniture, which are soft and spongy.

The study of sound is called *acoustics*. An understanding of acoustics is important if you want to have good hearing conditions in different spaces. For example, in large rooms such as churches, lecture rooms, and auditoriums, the ceilings are usually made smooth and hard so that sound in these rooms will be reflected to the listeners. Properly designed ceilings in large spaces can provide an adequate level of loudness for the room so that sound-amplifying systems such as public address systems will not be needed.

When quiet is needed in a room, sound-absorbing materials are added to the room. For example, in broadcast studios or recording studios, sound-absorbing materials are placed on the walls and ceilings to make these rooms particularly quiet. In another example, cars are often soundproofed to eliminate road noise. This is done by using soft, spongy materials that will absorb road noise and the noise that comes from the car's engine. Can you think of other uses for sound-absorbing materials?

RINGING GLASS

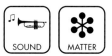

SOUND   MATTER

MATERIALS NEEDED

Plain drinking glass
(or glass jar)

Lead-crystal glass

Pencil

Place the plain drinking glass and the lead-crystal glass next to each other on a table or kitchen counter. With a pencil, gently tap the side of the plain drinking glass about 1 inch (2.5 cm) below the rim of the glass. Listen closely to the sound coming from the glass. Then gently tap the side of the lead-crystal glass about 1 inch below the rim of the glass, and listen closely to the sound coming from the glass.

You should find that the two glasses make different sounds when they are gently struck. The plain glass makes a dull sound that does not last very long. In contrast, the lead-crystal glass makes a clear and sharp ringing sound. This ringing sound from the lead-crystal glass should last for several seconds.

Common glass, like that found in inexpensive drinking glasses, jars, and windows, is made by heating a mixture of sand, limestone, and soda ash until it melts. This molten mixture is then formed into the desired shape and allowed to cool slowly. As the molten glass cools, it becomes hard.

Glass is a unique substance in that it is not a true solid. True solids are crystalline in structure. The building units of a true solid have a regularly repeating and ordered arrangement, like a stack of bricks. Examples of true solids are table sugar, table salt, and diamonds.

The building units in glass are less ordered, or more random, than the building units in a true solid. Glass can be thought of as both a solid and a liquid at the same time. Like a solid, glass shatters when struck hard. Like a liquid, glass can flow. This flow is extremely slow and does not become noticeable for many years. The windowpanes in very old houses often appear wavy. This is because the glass has flowed. If you measured the thickness of an old windowpane, you would find that it is thicker at the bottom than at the top due to the slow flow of the glass.

Lead-crystal glass is a special glass used to make fancy dinnerware and fancy glass pieces such as bowls, vases, and chandeliers. Another name for lead-crystal glass is *flint glass.*

Lead-crystal glass differs from ordinary glass in that a substance containing lead is substituted for the soda ash used in the common glass formula. The addition of lead makes the building units in crystal glass more ordered than the building units in ordinary glass. The lead in crystal glass also makes it heavier than regular glass.

Although still not a true solid, lead-crystal glass is more like a solid than is ordinary glass. Since lead-crystal glass is more solidlike, it vibrates more easily than does ordinary glass. This is why the crystal glass makes a lasting, clear ringing sound when it is gently struck and the plain glass makes a duller sound when it is struck.

In addition to being more solidlike, lead-crystal glass bends light rays much better than does ordinary glass. You can see this in lead crystal that has angular cuts in the glass. The glass sparkles with a brilliance. This is why lead-crystal glass is often used to make decorative glass pieces such as vases and chandeliers.

15

CONDUCTING ELECTRICITY WITH A PENCIL

MATERIALS NEEDED

Pliers

Pencil

Pencil sharpener

Wire cutters

Insulated wire, about 36 in. (91 cm) long

Lantern battery (6-volt)

Flashlight bulb

In this experiment you will see if a pencil can be used as part of an electric circuit to conduct, or carry, electricity.

Use a pair of pliers to break off the eraser end (both rubber and metal portion) of a wooden pencil. Then use a pencil sharpener to sharpen both ends of the pencil.

Use wire cutters to cut the insulated wire into three pieces, each about 12 in. (30 cm) in length. Remove almost 0.5 in. (about 1 cm) of insulation from both ends of the three pieces of wire. Connect one end of the first wire to the positive terminal of the battery (the 6-volt lantern type used in large flashlights). Wrap the other end of this wire around the point of one end of the pencil. Make sure the uninsulated end of the wire is on the pencil lead and not on the wooden part of the pencil. Wrap one end of the second wire around the point on the other end of the pencil. Attach one end of the third wire to the negative terminal of the battery.

As shown in Figure A, touch the two free ends of wire to the bottom and side of the flashlight bulb to complete the circuit. You

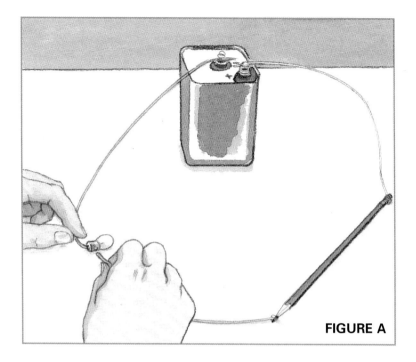

FIGURE A

should observe that the bulb gives off light. If it does not, try checking all your connections to make sure there are no loose wires. Now move the wires attached to the pencil lead at each end of the pencil to the wooden part of the pencil. What happens to the light when the circuit goes through the pencil wood?

Pencil lead is made of a pure form of carbon called *graphite* with clay added to it. Diamond is a different form of pure carbon. Graphite is an interesting substance because it can be used to write on paper and because it can conduct or carry electrons. Although graphite is not a metal, it can conduct electricity like a metal.

Graphite is made of a series of layers of linked carbon atoms that are stacked together. The carbon atoms in a layer are held tightly together. However, it is easy to separate one layer from another. Imagine a stack of books being spread across the floor. The books could easily slide past each other, and this would leave a line of books across the floor. In the same way, as a pencil is dragged across a page, layers of graphite slide past each other and leave a line of graphite spread on the page.

Graphite is a good conductor of electricity. Some electrons in graphite are locked into position holding atoms together, but other electrons are free to move through the solid. The battery is a source of extra electrons and provides the voltage potential to push electrons through the graphite. Even though diamond is also pure carbon, it is not made of layers, and it is not a good conductor of electricity.

When you moved the wires from the pencil lead (graphite) to the wooden shaft of the pencil, the flashlight bulb should have stopped glowing. The circuit was broken because wood does not conduct electricity. Metals and graphite can carry electrons, but diamond and wood do not allow electrons to flow through them.

Particles of graphite called *carbon black* are mixed with rubber and used to help strengthen the rubber used in making tires. Small pieces of graphite are also used as a lubricant because they are slippery and the layers of carbon will easily slide past each other. Although graphite is not a metal, it is used as an electrode to conduct electricity in the electrical process used to make aluminum from aluminum ore. Can you think of other possible uses of graphite?

16

ELECTRICITY AND SOLIDS

MATERIALS NEEDED

Wire cutters

Insulated wire, about 30 in. (76 cm) long

Lantern battery, 6-volt

Two large steel nails

Small jar, baby-food size

Flashlight bulb

Water

Measuring cup

Large drinking glass

Table salt

Teaspoon

Coffee filter

In this experiment you will explore how electricity can be used to help form solids.

Use wire cutters to cut the insulated wire into three pieces, each about 10 in. (25 cm) long. Remove about 1 in. (2.5 cm) of insulation from both ends of each of the three wires.

Connect one end of the first wire to the negative terminal of the battery (the 6-volt lantern type used in large flashlights). Tightly wrap the other end of this first wire around the head of a nail, and place the point of the nail down into the bottom of the small glass jar. Then connect one end of the second wire to the positive terminal of the battery. Wrap the other end of the second wire around the side of the flashlight bulb, as shown in Figure A. Finally, wrap one end of the third wire around the second nail and place the

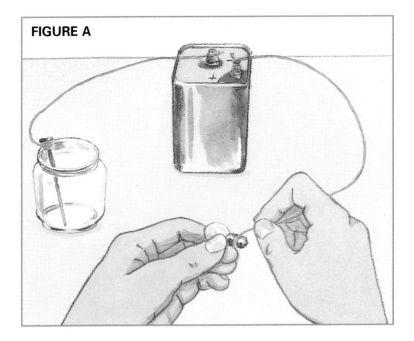

point of this nail down into the glass jar. Do not let the nails touch each other. The nails should be about 1 in. (2.5 cm) apart.

Run tap water at a sink for several minutes until the water is hot. Pour 1 cup (0.24 l) of hot tap water into a large drinking glass. Add 4 teaspoons (20 ml) of table salt to this glass. Stir this mixture for 1 minute, or until all the salt dissolves into the water. Pour enough of this salt water into the small glass jar to fill it about two-thirds full.

As shown in Figure B, touch the free end of the third wire to the bottom of the flashlight bulb. You should see the bulb light up as you complete the *circuit* (the path the electrons follow through the metal). If the bulb does not light up, check all the connections and make sure your battery is good.

Hold the wire on the bulb for about 3 minutes, and make sure the bulb stays lit the whole time. Watch the liquid in the glass jar. What do you see happening? Does something appear in the water?

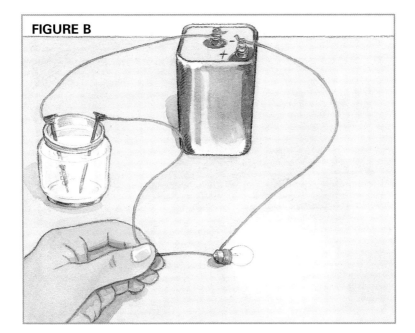

FIGURE B

As the electricity flows through the wires and the salt water, you should see gas bubbles being produced on the surface of the negative nail. You should also see a green solid form in the water. Smaller amounts of a brown solid may also appear. These solid particles are very small, and so they tend to float to the top of the salt water before slowly settling to the bottom of the jar.

Electrons flow from the negative terminal of the battery through the wire to the first nail. The extra electrons in the nail cause water molecules at the surface of the nail to produce hydrogen gas and negative hydroxide ions (OH⁻). Hydrogen gas causes the bubbles you see in the water.

As the electricity passes through the nail attached to the positive electrode, iron atoms in the nail are changed to positive iron ions that go into the salt water. Electrons are released in the metal as the ions are produced, and these electrons flow through the wire toward the battery to complete the circuit.

The iron ions that are released into the water can combine

with negative ions in the water such as chloride (Cl^-), hydroxide (OH^-), or even hypochlorite (ClO^-) to form solids that will not dissolve in the water. These solids, such as iron hydroxide or iron chloride, are what you see as a green solid that floats in the water.

You can try to filter out these solids by pouring the water and solid mixture through a coffee filter. Observe the solid that is left on the filter paper. How would you describe the solid you have collected on the filter paper?

Many important industrial chemicals are made by passing electricity through a mixture of ions in solution or hot molten solids made of ions. Examples of substances made in industry by using electricity include aluminum metal, sodium metal, chlorine gas, sodium hydroxide (caustic soda), magnesium metal, and hydrogen peroxide.

SCIENCE CONCEPTS

FURTHER READING

To explore further the properties of salts and solids:

Cooper, Christopher. *Matter.* New York: Dorling Kindersley, 1992.

Darling, David. *From Glasses to Gases: The Science of Matter.* New York: Dillon Press, 1992.

Kerrod, Robin. *Mineral Resources.* New York: Thomson Learning, 1994.

Mebane, Robert C., and Thomas R. Rybolt. *Adventures with Atoms and Molecules: Chemistry Experiments for Young People.* 4 vols. Hillside, New Jersey; Enslow, 1985–1992.

Peacock, Graham, and Cally Chambers. *The Super Science Book of Materials.* New York: Thomson Learning, 1993.

Symes, R. F., and Roger Harding. *Crystal and Gem.* New York: Knopf, 1991.

VanCleave, Janice. *Janice VanCleave's Chemistry for Every Kid.* New York: Wiley, 1989.

INDEX